WHO AM I?

by June Behrens

photographs by Ray Ambraziunas

ELK GROVE
PRESS, INC.

In appreciation to

June Claypool, the staff

and children of

Barton Hill School,

San Pedro, California.

WHO AM I?

by June Behrens

WHO AM I?

My name is Adriane.

I am my brother's sister.

I have short hair and I look pretty.

Everybody says I do.

WHO AM I?

I am Randolph.

I am strong.

I exercise.

I eat the right food.

WHO AM I?

Everybody calls me Inge.

My real name is Ingeborge.

I have a white rabbit.

Everyone wants to touch it.

WHO AM I?

Rafer is my name.

I help my Daddy wash his car.

He takes me to the beach.

WHO AM I?

I am Carlos.

I am a good citizen.

I am a handsome boy.

I am the best in sock ball.

I feel sad when someone gets hurt.

WHO AM I?

My name is Ofelia.

I want to learn to write in handwriting.

I like my friends in school.

WHO AM I?

Jiro is my name.

I am tall and straight.

I am always happy.

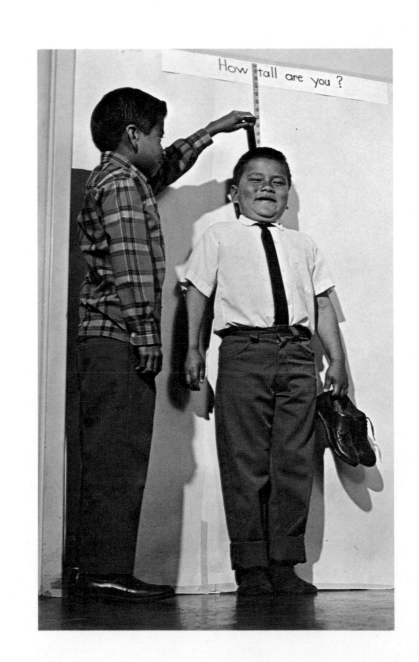

WHO AM I?

I am Pablo Diaz.

I do what the teacher says.

I can talk Spanish.

My teacher can not talk Spanish.

WHO AM I?

My name is Fumi.

I like to swing in the park.

My mother pushes me.

WHO AM I?

Perry is my name.

I like scary things.

I look like my brother Jerry.

We are twins.

WHO AM I?

I am Falacia.

I like to wear glasses.

I look like my mother.

I like to help my mother cook.

WHO AM I?

They call me Nathanial.

I am bad some times.

I like Carlos.

He is nice to people.

WHO AM I?

My name is Carmela.

We hatched some eggs.

A duck came out of my egg.

He grew fast!

WHO AM I?

I am a boy named Tak.

I look like a man.

I look like my father.

WHO AM I?

I am Booker.

I am big and I am six.

I am not afraid of dogs.

WHO AM I?

My name is Monica.

I know all the ABC's.

ABC's are the alphabet.

WHO AM I?

Irma is my name.

My daddy has a camera.

I smile.

He takes pictures of me.

WHO AM I?

I am Glenda.

Everyone likes my pony tails.

I like to plant seeds.

They grow into flowers.

WHO AM I?

WE ARE FIRST GRADERS.

WE LIVE IN THE UNITED STATES.

THE UNITED STATES IS IN AMERICA.

WE ARE ALL AMERICANS.